O N E

The seasons are passing at a ferocious pace!

—ONE

Manga creator ONE began *One-Punch Man* as a webcomic, which quickly went viral, garnering over 10 million hits. In addition to *One-Punch Man*, ONE writes and draws the series *Mob Psycho 100* and *Makai no Ossan*.

Y U S U K E M U R A T A

I believe I can solve 90 percent of my problems through sheer force of will.

—Yusuke Murata

A highly decorated and skilled artist best known for his work on *Eyeshield 21*, Yusuke Murata won the 122nd Hop Step Award (1995) for *Partner* and placed second in the 51st Akatsuka Award (1998) for *Samui Hanashi*.

ONE-PUNCH MAN | 28

ONE + YUSUKE MURATA

☆THE STORIES, CHARACTERS, AND INCIDENTS

MENTIONED IN THIS PUBLICATION
ARE ENTIRELY FICTIONAL.

SAITAMA

FLASHY FLASH

TANK-TOP MASTER

ATOMIC SAMURAI

MUMEN RIDER

OCULETTE

CHILD EMPEROR

GENOS

CHARACTERS

CONTENTS

ONE-PUNCH MAN VOL.28

STORY

Gyoro-Gyoro, the supposed brains of the Monster Association, is revealed to be a decoy for the psychic Psychos, the true mastermind. Finding herself on the losing end of a fierce battle against Tornado, Psychos fuses with the Monster King Orochi and accesses unbelievable power. A frightful battle between psychics ensues. Seeing an opening, Psychos delivers a grievous wound to Tornado.

However, Genos arrives to assist Tornado, thereby earning Psychos's wrath. Meanwhile, Saitama is digging out Flashy Flash from a mound of rubble in the underground labyrinth…

PUNCH 138: **THE WRINGER**

GUDOM

WHSH

JASHANK

KTUNK

BTONK

KRUNK

RISE AND SHINE!

GASP!

GRNK

GYAH!

GWUNK

TOONK

GOT 'EM!

KYAH!

KYAH!

GRLASH!

GUH!

KRAKL

!!

KRAKL

KRAKL

FINALLY, I CAN FOCUS ON THIS FIGHT!

HEH...

I DID NOT DO IT FOR YOU.

WELL DONE, DEMON CYBORG.

HWOOM

YOU SAID SOMETHING EARLIER.

NGH!

YOUR NAME...

...A SINGLE FINGER!!

I CAN'T MOVE...

GR

NCH

HWISH

...IS PSYCHOS, RIGHT?

YOU THREAT-ENED MY SISTER.

MY SISTER'S CONCENTRATION HAS IMPROVED!

IS HER PSYCHIC ABILITY LIMITLESS?

THE POWER UP THERE IS INCREASING!

....!

WHOA...

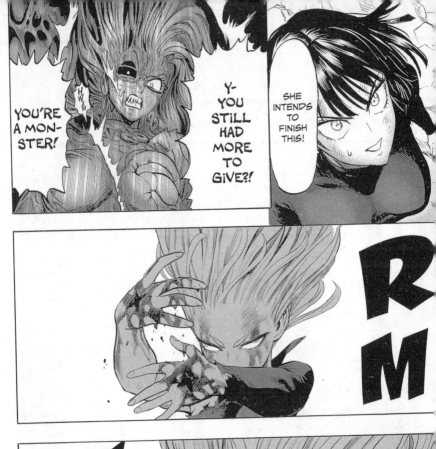

YOU'RE A MON-STER!

Y-YOU STILL HAD MORE TO GIVE?!

SHE INTENDS TO FINISH THIS!

HMM?

NO
...

...

A TECH-NICAL GLITCH?

OPERATOR, THE MAP OF CITY Z IS WARPING.

GRRRRR!?

THE *CITY* IS BEING TWISTED.

THEY'RE BLEEDING!

...SO YOU GOTTA WRING IT OUT!

AN OLD RAG CAN ABSORB A LOT...

GRUNK

?!

OH NO ...

KTHUD THUD

PIG GOD!

RUMMMBLE

....?!

!

TORNADO?

BLRFT

...

OUR BARRIER FADED.

FWSH

HM?

IS MY SISTER ALL RIGHT?!

A DISRUP-TION TO HER PSYCHIC WAVES?!

DID I USE TOO MUCH POWER AT ONCE?

PANG

KOFF

PANG

WHAT?! WHY NOW?!

THIS IS OUR CHANCE!

SHE SUDDENLY LET UP!

SMOKE SCREEN!

SPWOO

?!

KRAK

PWOP

SNAP

I'LL SUCK BLOOD FROM THE CITY'S INHABITANTS!

THIS SMOKE IS GOOEY!

GWooooo

EW
...

...?!

I SENSE HER IN MANY DIRECTIONS!!

HA HA HA! I LEARNED A NEW TRICK!

FORTUNE IS ON MY SIDE!

EVEN TERRIBLE TORNADO HAS LIMITS!

SIMPLY MAIN-TAINING THAT BARRIER WILL KEEP YOU BUSY!

HEH!

GA WP

...I'LL SPEAR YOU THROUGH THE HEART!

PWOOM

SHOOM

PSS

ULP
...

BSHOOM

FOUND YOU!

NGH!

NOW WHAT ?!

WHAT'S THAT?

THERE'S ANOTHER AIRCRAFT!

THAT CREEP'S ALIVE?!

IS THAT DRIVE KNIGHT?

GWOOOSH

GWAWWW

LOWER ORGANISMS CANNOT STAND AGAINST...

ANOTHER HERO?!

...THE APEX OF EVOLUTION!

THE ESSENCE OF EVOLUTION IS CONFLICT!

VIEEE

AND I ASK FOR YOUR SUPPORT.

BLECH...

TCH... NO TIME FOR STANDING AROUND. IT'S OUT OF RANGE, BUT I'LL TRY MY FLYING SWORD!

HUH?

WHSH

TH

WSH

GLORP GLORP

BLORFF

YUCK!

PIG GOD!

YOU PRO-TECTED EVERYONE INSIDE YOUR STOMACH ?!

SPLOOOOOSH

WHAT THE?!

IT LOOKS LIKE YOU DIGESTED ZOMBIE-MAN!!

POK POK

NO, I'M JUST WOUNDED...

GAAAAAH!!

W-WHERE AM I?

GASP!

PIG GOD...

THE OTHER SWORDS-MEN ARE ALL RIGHT TOO.

IT WAS EASY BECAUSE YOU GATHERED EVERYONE IN ONE PLACE.

KLANK

PHEW...

Aw, it was nothing.

HOW CAN I THANK YOU?!

OH...

I'M STILL A LONG WAY FROM CLASS S...

I AM DEEPLY GRATE-FUL!

...I SEE...

I NEED ANOTHER WAY.

I CAN'T REACH.

CLUMP

IAI!

!

M....

MASTER!

SOMEHOW...
I SURVIVED!

WELL
DONE!

...

CLASP

YES, THANKS TO A LIFT FROM YOU.

MASTER, I'M GLAD YOU CAME.

?

HM?

HEEEY! OVER HERE!

WE'VE GOT WOUNDED!

LOOK!

THE RESCUE HELI-COPTER!

EVA-
SIVE
AC-
TION
!!

THERE'S AN INVISIBLE WALL THERE!

THERE'S A BARRIER?!

THAT WAS CLOSE!

ULP...

THE SITUATION HAS REACHED **EXTREME** PROPOR-TIONS.

IT'S MASSIVE!

THRUM
THRUM

A BARRIER... IS TORNADO HERE?

...

STAY HERE AND CONTINUE THE RESCUE OP!

I NEED TO GIVE HER BACK-UP!

MUMEN RIDER!

HUH?

UH, YEAH.

LIGHTNING MAX, IS TORNADO AT THAT TOWER?

TUMP

KRUNK

GWUP

I'M GONNA MAKE IT SO YOU CAN CARRY OUT THE WOUNDED SOON!

BE CAREFUL.

UNDER-STOOD.

YOU TOO!

Hw **O** o o

....!!

MAYBE I SHOULD WEAR ONE TOO...

DOES HIS TANK-TOP HAVE ANYTHING TO DO WITH THAT...?

VREEE BABOOSH

FWOOSH

ALL RIGHT, BACK TO RESCUING PEOPLE!

COOPER-ATION, HUH?

PUNCH 140:
DISGRACE AND FOUNDATION

Five minutes ago...

...AND NOW TERRIBLE TORNADO IS BATTLING THE MONSTER ASSOCIATION'S LEADER!

RMMM RMMM

A TOWER SPLIT THE EARTH'S CRUST AND ROSE OVERHEAD...

I'D LIKE TO TAKE SAMPLES OF THE FLESH LYING AROUND, BUT I'M LOW ON ENERGY.

KRAKL KRAKL

KRAKRAKL

FWAA

SO I'LL HELP MYSELF!

TOMP

THIS IS JUST WHAT I NEED.

VMM

I'M STILL NO MATCH FOR UGLINESS!!

IN THE END, ALL I COULD DO WAS COVER MY EYES AND COWER LIKE A BABY!

...BUT NOW LOOK AT ME!

I TALKED BIG BEFORE JOINING THIS FIGHT...

HUH ?!

DID THEY OVERHEAR ME PANICKING TO TORNADO OVER MY TRANSMITTER?!

GASP

WHY ARE THEY STARING AT ME?

URGH...

HOW DARE THEY LOOK AT ME—A TRUE HERO—WITH ANYTHING BUT ENVY!!

THOSE SCUMBAGS!

YOU DON'T LOOK WELL, SO MAYBE YOU SHOULD JOIN THE REAR GUARD.

UH... HI, AMAI.

THE BRAT! HE'S ONLY ADDING TO MY SHAME!!

IS HE TREATING ME WITH PITY?!

I BET SEKINGAR OVERHEARD TOO...

ME? IN THE REAR GUARD?

THANKS.

BUT I ACCEPT YOUR PROPOSAL.

ONLY A CHILD WOULD SPEAK SO FOOLISHLY!

I OF ALL PEOPLE DO NOT DESERVE THIS!!

OH, THE DISGRACE!!

...IT WILL RUIN THE SUPERSTAR STATUS I HAVE WORKED SO HARD TO ATTAIN.

IF WORD OF THIS REACHES HERO ASSOCIATION HEADQUARTERS...

I MUST COVER UP MY FAILURE.

...DUE TO A COWARDLY MONSTER'S ATTACK FROM THE REAR!

NO ONE WOULD FIND IT SUSPICIOUS IF EVERYONE HERE WERE TO DIE...

MWA HA HA ...

NNNGH... URNGH!

WHAT'S WRONG ?!

HEY, STOP THAT!

BAM BAM

ARRRGH!

I CAN HANDLE THIS.

SPARE ME YOUR CONCERN.

HUFF!

HUFF!

...OF BEING COOL.

I ALMOST FORGOT THE FOUNDA- TION...

THAT'S WHY YOU'RE SO UPSET?

I JUST NOTICED MY OUTFIT ISN'T WELL COORDINATED

PUNCH 141:
UNCONQUERABLE

GARO DEFEATED YOU?!

HOW CAN ANYONE EVEN BEAT THIS GUY?

YOU DIDN'T WIN? IN HAND-TO-HAND COMBAT?!

THERE MAY BE NO ONE WHO CAN STOP HIM.

...SO HE'LL REAPPEAR SOON.

GARO IS ALIVE...

I DON'T UNDERSTAND IT!

...STRONGER AND FIERCER THAN EVER!

N-NO MATTER WHAT YOU DO, HE GETS BACK UP...

...THE KIND OF EVIL I WANT TO COMMIT.

YES... I JUST REALIZED...

MAYBE IT'S JUST DUE TO THAT HUMAN MEATBALL'S PUNCHES, BUT MY HEAD FEELS CLEARER!

BUT WHAT'S HAPPENING TO ME? THE MORE I GET BEATEN DOWN, THE STRONGER I GET!

...THAT I CAN REACH THREAT LEVEL GOD!

NOW I'M CONFIDENT...

...I'LL CAST THE HUMAN RACE INTO AN ABYSS OF FEAR!

AND THEN...

EVERYONE EVERYWHERE WILL CRINGE IN FEAR...

...IN THANKFULNESS AT SIMPLY BEING ALIVE.

...AND JOIN HANDS...

BULLYING AND DISCRIMINATION...

...AND EVEN WAR.

IN A WORLD WHERE MERE SURVIVAL IS A STRUGGLE, EVIL DEEDS WILL VANISH.

INJUSTICE AND THOSE RESPONSIBLE FOR IT WILL DISAPPEAR.

THE SNOTTY BRAT?!

H-HOW WERE YOU ABLE TO FIND ME?

OLD DUDE!

I'M A LOSER.

I BROKE.

TREMBLE

PLIP

PLIP

I...

LUSTER...

I ALSO HAD...

...AN AWFUL REALIZATION.

AND I DIDN'T JUST LOSE.

I DON'T ACTUALLY CARE ABOUT JUSTICE OR—

I UNDER-STAND YOUR ANGER.

AMAI MASK ...

HEY!

WE DON'T NEED COWARDS HERE, SO GET LOST!

ARE YOU A HERO OR NOT?!

SELF-PITY! WHINING! AND EXCUSES!

I'M TRULY SORRY.

BUT WEREN'T YOU ALSO FALLING APART EARLIER?

...YOU...

SUPER-ALLOY BLACK-LUSTER...

HEY, YOU HAVE NO RIGHT TO—

YOU'RE STILL A HUNK OF MUSCLE! AND SUPER-STRONG!

B-BUT EVEN THOSE KICKS FROM AMAI DIDN'T HURT YOU!

WE WILL DEFINITELY NEED YOUR STRENGTH...

GARO AND THE LEADERS OF THE MONSTER ASSOCIATION ARE STILL ALIVE.

...TO BEAT THEM!

NO, NOT REALLY.

DON'T **YOU** HAVE ANYONE TO PROTECT?!

I FIGHT TO PROTECT MY BUDDIES IN THE CLINK!

OH, YES ...

... YOU DO!

YOU WANT ...

...TO PROTECT **YOUR-SELF!**

AND I THINK THAT'S GREAT!

EVERY PERSON IS DEAREST TO THEMSELVES! YOU'VE BUILT—AND PROTECTED—YOURSELF!

BUT NOW YOU'RE JUST GONNA COWER?

DO THAT AND YOU'LL LOSE WHO'S MOST IMPORTANT! YOUR-SELF!

...AND SEE HOW IT TREM-BLES.

LOOK AT YOUR BODY...

I'M
THE
SAME
WAY.

I'VE
ENCOUN-
TERED
DIFFICULTIES
...

...
AND I'VE DISAP-POINTED MYSELF...

...BUT I GET BACK UP AND KEEP MOVING FORWARD.

THAT'S
WHAT
HEROES
DO.

WHAT DOES YOUR **PRIDE** SAY?

SO TELL ME!

TRMBL TRMBL

N N N G H ...

GET UP OR I'LL DEEP KISS YOU.

N N N G H ...

IN THAT CASE...

...WE SHOULD COOPERATE IN TAKING THAT THING DOWN!!

...

YOU WANT TO COOPERATE?!

HUH?!

SHALL I STRIKE YOU ALL DOWN?

CAREFUL WHAT YOU EAT.

HAVE YOU EATEN SOMETHING WEIRD?

YOU'D PUT YOUR BUTT IN OUR HANDS?!

YOU? THE HIGH-AND-MIGHTY WARRIOR?

JUST THIS ONCE! AND ONLY BECAUSE I RECOGNIZE THEIR STRENGTH!

HMPH!

What changed?

MASTER!!

HM?

WHAT DO YOU HAVE IN MIND?

P O T
P O T

IS TERRIBLE TORNADO UP THERE?

HWOMP

I CAME TO LEND SUPPORT!

TANK-TOP MASTER!

WHAT'S THE SITUATION?

GLOMP

HM?

WELCOME BACK!!

I THINK IT'S GONNA WORK OUT.

AMAI
MASK
...

...BUT
I'VE
CHANGED
MY MIND.

I
THOUGHT
YOU
WERE
ALL
TALK...

HA
HA
HA!

YOU
REALLY
ARE
CREEPY...

WHY
NOW?

...

I NEVER THOUGHT THEY WOULD COOPERATE.

THEY REALLY **ARE** CLASS-S HEROES!

THEY RAN INTO A WALL, BUT GREW AND FOUND A NEW WAY FORWARD!

NO, DON'T FIGHT!

DON'T WORRY, AWRY MASK.

...BUT DON'T HOLD ME BACK.

I DON'T EXPECT MUCH FROM A GUY THE ENEMY **DENUDED**...

PUNCH 142:
RESONANCE

HELLO.

TU⌣P

MIND IF **WE** JOIN?

WHAT A COINCIDENCE.

GRIN

WHAT?!

GOOD QUESTION. AFTER ALL, YOU **EXCLUDED** ME FROM THE MISSION.

W-WHAT ARE YOU DOING HERE?!

BANG?!

BANG!

YEAH, W-WELL...

...I HAD A REASON FOR THAT.

YOU SAID HE WASN'T PARTICIPATING BECAUSE YOU COULDN'T REACH HIM.

WHAT DOES HE MEAN, CHILD EMPEROR?

HEH... GIVEN MY RECORD, PERHAPS THAT'S UNDERSTAND-ABLE.

YOU WERE WORRIED THAT I'D GO SOFT ON GARO BECAUSE HE'S A FORMER PUPIL.

I WILL TAKE RESPON-SIBILITY BY DEFEATING HIM WITH MY OWN FISTS.

BUT DO NOT WORRY.

SO REMOVING ME FROM THE MISSION WAS FOR THE BEST. I OWE YOU ONE, BOY.

ACTUALLY, I **PREFER** SETTLING THIS AS HIS FORMER MASTER TO DOING SO AS A HERO.

I'LL HELP IN ANY WAY I CAN!

PLEASE! WE MUST HURRY IF WE'RE TO HELP MY SISTER!!

HELLISH BLIZZARD ...

...

I SUSPECT MY SISTER IS ALREADY UNCONSCIOUS!!

BWOOM

TCH!

SHE'S UNCONSCIOUS.

TORNADO...

WHO...?

YOU SHOULDN'T INTERFERE.

...THAT SOMEONE WILL COME HELP.

DON'T GIVE ME HOPE...

...at a certain research facility.

Eighteen years ago...

GRARRRRRR

RUUUN!

GYAAAH! A SYNTHETIC BEAST BROKE FREE!!

VREEE

VREEE

LET ME OUT OF HERE!

DON'T LEAVE ME!

WAIT!

101

ALL PERSONNEL, EVACUATE!

TROMP

TROMP

PRIORITIZE SAVING SUBJECTS WITH GREATER PROMISE!

YES, SIR!

NO! HER NUMBERS HAVE LEVELED OFF!

DIRECTOR! THAT GIRL!

FWOO

KLOMP

...SO THIS IS JUST FOR FUN.

I USUALLY WORK AT A JOB JUST LIKE ANYONE ELSE, THOUGH...

WHY DIDN'T YOU USE YOUR **POWER?**

HERO?

NO, YOU'RE **LYING.**

...I CAN'T USE IT ANY-MORE.

UM...

...THAT THEY MIGHT LET YOU OUT OF HERE.

YOU THOUGHT IF YOU SUPPRESSED YOUR **POWER**...

NO ONE IN HERE OR OUT THERE NEEDS ME.

IT DOESN'T MATTER ANY- MORE.

MAMA AND PAPA **SOLD** ME!

YOUR DEAR LITTLE SISTER.

NO, SOMEONE **DOES** NEED YOU.

PAT

YOU MUST PROTECT YOUR FAMILY.

THOSE WHO POSSESS GREAT POWER...

OKAY? LET ME GIVE YOU SOME ADVICE.

IT WOULD'VE BEEN EASIER FOR ME TO GET A SAMPLE IF SHE HAD BEEN OFF THE MARK A BIT.

TORNADO IS SUCH A BEAST!

BUT IT'S ALL DAMAGED ON A CELLULAR LEVEL!

IT DUG INTO THE EARTH LIKE ROOTS, HUH?

ARE THESE...

...THE REMAINS OF THE MONSTER KING?

HWUP

DEMON CYBORG!

HWO...

URGH!

EXCEL-LENT!

KLANK

GWOOSH

PUNCH 143: INTO THE ABYSS

BOOM

HAH!

BOOSH

GAME OVER!

UH... YOU'RE WELCOME.

BUT I DIDN'T DO ANYTHING TO THE TANK TOP...

THANKS, MISS BLIZZARD!

MY TANK TOP IS SUDDENLY PROVIDING INCREASED AGILITY! I DIDN'T KNOW YOU HAD THAT POWER!

WOOOOOO

DEMON CYBORG...

KSHNK

I WANT TO COMBINE WITH YOU AND INTEGRATE OUR POWER CORES FOR MAXIMUM OUTPUT.

I'M RUNNING LOW ON ENERGY.

...I REQUEST YOUR ASSISTANCE.

THEN
HERE
GOES!

...ARE
YOU
WITH
ME?

IT
MAY
NOT
WORK,
BUT...

VREEEEEET

CAUTION

POWER CORE NEAR
DEPLETION

YES,
I AM
WITH
YOU.

VMM

HA! YOU'LL HAVE TO DO BETTER THAN HURL DEBRIS!

DRIVE KNIGHT, MY CORE COULD EXPLODE AT ANY MOMENT!

AT MY SIGNAL, SEPARATE IMMEDIATELY! UNDERSTOOD?

...PIECES OF JUNK!

YOU...

NOW'S YOUR CHANCE!

SHE STOPPED MOVING!

UMPH!

VICTORY IS **OURS.**

DARK
☆
ANGEL
☆
RUSH!

VIBRATION ☆

!!

FLOWING WATER!

WHIRLING WIND!

THOOM

FWAM

THEY DID IT!

HUH?

NO, NOT YET.

BIG SIS?

GOOD! JUST A LITTLE MORE!

OH, YOU MEAN THIS?

IF ONLY IT COULD BE MOVED...

NO, THERE'S SOMETHING IMMENSELY HEAVY THERE.

CAN'T YOU GET **YOURSELF** OUT NOW?

WHAT **IS** THIS?

WHEW!

CRUNK

BETTER NOW?

YES, THANKS!

TOSS

SHOULD I **PULL** YOU?

W-WHAT IS THIS THING?

UGH!!

YIKES!!

NO, STAY BACK!

YOU MIGHT BREAK SOMETHING!

KTHUNK!

I'M IN A DELICATE SITUATION HERE!

TCH!

MORE INTENSE RUMBLING...

RMMM

WAH!

RMMM

KRUMBL

KRUMBL

FLASH-
KILL...

Flash-
kill

WELL,
BOULDERS
AREN'T
GONNA
BREAK
MY **ARM**.

USE
YOUR
HEAD.

**THAT'S
WHAT YO**
**WERE
WORRIED
ABOUT
BREAKIN**
?!

THAT MUST BE TORNADO!

I SEE A GREEN LIGHT!

A LANCE OF LIGHT...

!!

SHNK

SO LONG!

NO.

I SHOULD HAVE JUST BLASTED THE WALL APART IF IT WAS GOING TO BREAK ANYWAY.

ARE YOU INSULTING MY SWORD?

FLASH-KILL SURE DIDN'T COME **OUT** IN A FLASH!

SNEAK

HM?

...

THIS'S MY CHANCE TO SLIP AWAY!

GWUP

WO

OOOOO

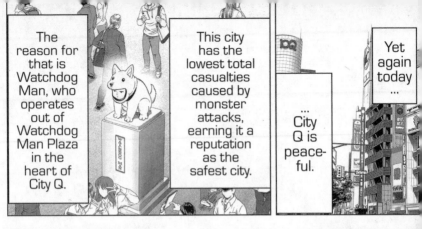

The reason for that is Watchdog Man, who operates out of Watchdog Man Plaza in the heart of City Q.

This city has the lowest total casualties caused by monster attacks, earning it a reputation as the safest city.

Yet again today ...

... City Q is peaceful.

I'M SLEEPY.

YAWN

BONUS MANGA: SENSE OF SMELL

Whether attacks come by air...

...his sharp sense of smell immediately detects the monsters. He zips over at superspeed estimated at 250 kilometers per hour and dispatches the ne'er-do-wells within minutes.

...or from underground...

?!

He has even defeated monsters dozens of kilometers away before the local police could react.

That day, attacks came from multiple monsters estimated to be threat level Demon.

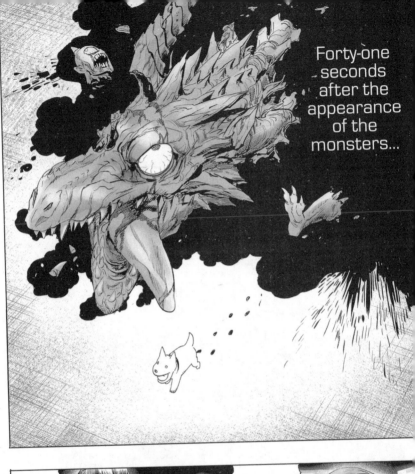

Forty-one seconds after the appearance of the monsters...

NOW WE CAN'T ASSIGN A THREAT LEVEL.

FORGET BACKUP. CALL IN *CLEAN-UP.*

WATCHDOG MAN KILLED THEM ALL...

...BEFORE WE COULD SOUND THE ALARM!

Yet again today, City Q is peaceful thanks to Watchdog Man.

...his full power.

And still no one knows...

28 Into the Abyss (End)

ONE-PUNCH MAN
VOLUME 28
SHONEN JUMP EDITION

STORY BY | ONE
ART BY | YUSUKE MURATA

TRANSLATION | JOHN WERRY
TOUCH-UP ART AND LETTERING | JAMES GAUBATZ
DESIGN | PAUL PADURARIU
EDITOR | JOHN BAE

ONE-PUNCH MAN © 2012 by ONE, Yusuke Murata
All rights reserved.
First published in Japan in 2012 by SHUEISHA Inc., Tokyo.
English translation rights arranged by SHUEISHA Inc.

Printed in the U.S.A.

Published by VIZ Media, LLC
P.O. Box 77010
San Francisco, CA 94107

10 9 8 7 6 5 4 3 2 1
First printing, May 2024

VIZ MEDIA
viz.com

SHONEN JUMP